Too Small!

Christine Finochio • Jennette MacKenzie

The sun is up. It's spring. Rita is happy because spring means it is time to play baseball.

Rita opens her closet doors and looks for her baseball shoes. She finds them.
She tries them on. Her foot gets stuck.
She pushes and pushes, but her foot won't go in! Too small!

"Oh, well," says Rita. "I'll try on my baseball uniform."

She tries to put on the shirt, but her head gets stuck. She can't put it on. She looks at the shorts. They look too small, too. "Did they shrink in the dryer?" Rita asks.

Rita goes into the bathroom. She looks for her mouth guard.

She finds it and puts it into her mouth.

Oh, no! It doesn't fit!

Then she remembers—she lost her two front teeth last week!

Rita goes downstairs to the closet where she keeps her baseball hat. She tries on her hat. It doesn't fit. It's too small!

"Mom, I can't go to baseball! Nothing fits me!" shouts Rita.

Mom comes upstairs and looks at Rita's baseball things. Mom smiles.

Mom calls Fong, the girl next door.

"Do you play baseball?" asks Mom.

"Yes, I do," says Fong. Fong comes over. Mom gives Fong all of Rita's baseball things. Fong is so happy.

"Thank you, Rita," she says.

Mom says to Rita,

"Now that you are bigger, we need to get you bigger things."

"I have grown since last summer," says Rita.

"Yes, you have," says Mom.